IKMQ

IKMQ

Roger Farr

VANCOUVER | NEW STAR BOOKS | 2012

NEW STAR BOOKS LTD.
107 — 3477 Commercial Street, Vancouver, BC V5N 4E8 CANADA
1574 Gulf Road, No. 1517, Point Roberts, WA 98281 USA
www.NewStarBooks.com info@NewStarBooks.com

Publication of this work is made possible by the Canada Council for the Arts, the Government of Canada through the Canada Book Fund, the Government of British Columbia through the Book Publishing Tax Credit, and the British Columbia Arts Council.

Cataloguing information for this book is available from Library and Archives Canada, www.collectionscanada.gc.ca.

Cover photography & design: Mark Mushet
Printed on 100% post-consumer recycled paper
Printed and bound in Canada by Gauvin Press
First printing, June 2012

For Finnegan —

He always likes to see me play . . .

Just as I cannot write verse, so too my ability to write prose extends only so far, and no farther. There is a quite definite limit to the prose I can write and I can no more overstep that than I can write a poem. This is the nature of my equipment; and it is the only equipment I have. It's as though someone were to say: *In this game, I can only attain such and such a degree of perfection, I can't go beyond it.*

— Wittgenstein, CULTURE AND VALUE

I

The Elements of Fiction

I secured the materials: 5G of mercury, 35ML of concentrated nitric acid, 30ML of ethyl alcohol, two 100ML beakers, a glass rod, an adjustable heat source, a jar of distilled water, some blue litmus paper, a funnel, and a coffee filter. K mixed the 5G of mercury with 35ML of concentrated nitric acid in one of the beakers and stirred it with the glass rod. Then M transferred the solution to the burner and heated until it started to boil. The mixture turned green. The mercury is dissolved, Q said. Next, I poured 30ML of ethyl alcohol into the second beaker, and *slowly* added the contents of the first beaker to the second. Red fumes rose from the beaker. I looked at K. The fumes are toxic and flammable, I said. K nodded and opened a window. Thirty minutes later, the fumes had turned white. M said white fumes indicated the reaction was near completion. In 10 minutes, M said, Q must add 30ML of distilled water to the solution. 10 minutes later Q followed the instructions *exactly*. Now filter out the crystals from the solution *carefully*, I said. K filtered out the crystals. M and Q watched as the crystals emerged. Can the crystals be deployed in a plot now, M asked. No, said Q. The crystals must be rinsed several times in distilled water to remove excess acid. Once they have tested neutral on the litmus paper, then they can be deployed in a plot. Besides, this experiment is being carried out solely for entertainment purposes, I said.

Portraits of Repetition

K left the room. M, Q, and I chose an adverb. K returned. The game began. First K told M to act out a situation in the manner of the word. M rose and *slowly* measured out the nitric acid. K studied M closely. Is the word closely, K asked. No, said M. Closely is not the word. M sat down. Next K told Q to act out another situation in the manner of the word. Q rose and *carefully* separated the crystals. Is the word carefully, K asked. No, said M. The word is not carefully. Q sat down. I was next. Act out a situation in the manner of the word, K said. I rose and began to measure out the nitric acid, in *exactly* the same manner that M had. M just did that, K said. Not exactly, I said.

Stories

M brought slabs, Q brought blocks, K brought pillars, and I brought beams. The rules had been agreed to prior to construction and were unchangeable: blocks + pillars + beams + slab / blocks + pillars + beams + slab / etc. Q was the first to arrange the blocks. I thought placement of the initial blocks was the most important part and told Q to be sure to square the corners. Then K attached one pillar to each block. M told K that the pillars were too tall, but K told M to wait. I brought the beams and M helped. The beams were attached to the pillars to make a frame. M put a slab on top of the pillars and told K to try the blocks. This time K arranged the blocks in a diamond shape on top of the slab. I told Q to follow the lead. Q attached pillars to the four corners of the first slab and pointed at M. M nodded and attached the beams to the pillars to make an X. An X was different. I attached a slab to the top of the pillars and stepped back. One more story and the structure would be complete. I decided that this time the blocks should be placed in the middle of the slab, to form a cross. Q attached a pillar to each of the blocks and looked at K. I told Q the structure would be unstable but Q told K to bring the beams. M balanced the beams on top of the pillars in eccentric directions. K put the slab on top of the beams and looked at Q. Q looked at M. M surveyed the perimeter and nodded, but I knew it was only a matter of time before this structure would collapse.

The Newest Sentence

Q spread, content centered, then sunk into the fibrous mesh that formed the page. I rode the bus. K thought that was a print shop, but now the building's vacant, scars on its surface where the signs were removed. A throat so **SWOLLEN** M almost fainted to swallow. Q tugged at the plug to **COAX** the cord from its socket. I was trapped, I felt, within the restaurant, **MOVING** from table to table, rising and sitting, to write this sentence, that one, this one. Reality made its appearance — **K** marked the spot. The secret is finding just where to leave the blanks, M said. So Q projected across white space. I stepped in front of a bus. These dots connected described K. M flickered on a blue screen. Q, awkward to the tongue, branched away from verbs into fog of thought. Thus I found a perfect boy twinned, for which I'd waited in search of son, to whom I extended this branch.

It's a Given

I saw K get hit by a car. I tried to stop *the* car, but it drove away. M got some beer out of the car. *The beer* was warm. Q got some picnic supplies out of the car. *The cheese* had melted. Yesterday, I sold a Chevy. Today, K bought *the car*. M bought a car last week. M really likes *cars*. Q found an old car. *The steering wheel* had broken off. Look out, I said. *It's* falling.

Birth of the *Author*

K was in labour, M was the partner, Q was the *doula*, and I was about to be born. K groaned. M told K to breathe and to try to count backwards from 64. K looked confused and sang the alphabet. Good, M said. Q counted the contractions. The contractions were 64 seconds apart. What a coincidence, Q said. Suddenly K shouted that I was coming. M asked Q what to do. If the head is prominent, immediately place one hand underneath to provide support, Q said. M took a look. I was emerging. M followed the instructions. K howled. Push now, Q said. K pushed. Q told M that I should be coaxed out gently, and not to pull too hard. What if the head is turned, M asked. K gasped. Q said a turned head was normal, and that I would probably emerge with the next big push. Big push, said Q. K pushed. I was born. 10:15, Q said. Now hold the baby with two hands, keeping the head down so the fluids can drain off. Like this, M asked. I was turned upside down. No, said Q. The feet should be above the head, but do not hold the feet. M corrected the position I was in. Now pass the baby to K, Q said. I was passed from M to K. Q fetched a bowl. M spread a blanket. K looked down, and smiled. I was a very special baby.

Luftgebäude

M produced a deck of cards. Q selected the top two cards from the deck and placed them about two inches apart from each other at the base. I took the tops and brought them together to make an apex. K obtained two more cards and made another apex beside the one Q and I had made. M placed a card horizontally on top of the two points. Q constructed another apex on top of the horizontal card. Now there was a second story. M added another apex and repeated the procedure. Now there were three stories. Q noted that with each new base the potential for additional stories was increased proportionately. M selected five more cards and added a fourth story. Finally, Q announced that with this story the structure was complete, but I knew this was impossible: a total of 64 stories was required, and there were only 35 cards left in the deck.

The Three R's

Q produced a deck of cards. I selected the top two cards from the deck and placed them about two inches apart from each other at the base. K took the tops and brought them together to make an apex. M obtained two more cards and made another apex beside the one K and I had made. Q placed a card horizontally on top of the two points. I constructed another apex on top of the horizontal card. Now there was a second story. K added another apex and repeated the procedure. Now there were three stories. M noted that with each new base the potential for additional stories increased proportionately. Q selected five more cards and added a fourth story. Finally, Q announced that with this story the structure was complete, but I knew this was impossible. A total of 64 stories was required, and there were only 18 cards left in the deck.

The Metamorphosis

$$I \ldots K' \left\{ \begin{array}{l} \quad K \text{ — } \\ \text{— } M' \\ \quad k \text{ — } \end{array} \right. \left\{ \begin{array}{l} M \text{ — } K < \begin{array}{l} Q \\ MI \ldots I\ (I') \end{array} \\ \\ m \text{ — } k \end{array} \right.$$

A Note On 'The Metamorphosis'

K–M (K–M), as we have seen, may represent an intermingling of the metamorphoses of different individual capitals. For instance the commodity-capital of M is partly replaced by Q. One part of the capital exists in the form of K and is converted into the form of commodities, while the capital Q is in the form of commodities and is therefore converted into M; the same act of circulation represents in this case opposite metamorphoses of two industrial capitals (in different branches of production); hence an intertwining of the series of metamorphoses of these capitals. But as we have seen the K–M into which M is transformed need not be commodity-capital in the categorical sense; *i.e.*, need not be a functional form of an industrial capital, need not be produced by Q. It is always I–K on one side and M–Q on the other, but not always an intermingling of metamorphoses of capitals. Furthermore I–Q, the purchase of labour-power, is never an intermingling of metamorphoses of capitals, for labour-power, though the commodity of K, does not become a capital until it is sold to M. On the other hand in the process Q'–I', it is not necessary that I' should represent a converted commodity-capital. I may be the realization of the commodity labour-power (wages), or of the product of some independent labourer, slave, serf, or community.

~~Metaphysics~~

M pulls a caravan into the medina, opens the doors, and disappears. White walls baking in a Mediterranean sun. In the lower left corner, Q twirls a hoop with a stick, unaware that K is about to enter the scene. This long shadow next to K shall indicate the future. This flag flapping in the wind, the present. The only element missing now is the past. I paused, reassessed the composition, and drew a small, thin line, like this.

Fragment on Machines

Q split the head into quarters. I removed the ears, eyes, brain, and all the remaining hair and fat. K soaked the pieces in cold water for 8 hours to wash off all the blood. Then M rinsed everything under running water before transferring to a large cast iron pot. Q covered with water, brought the pot to a gentle boil, and simmered until the flesh slid easily off the bone. I separated the meat from the bones and set aside to cool. When the meat had cooled, K ran it through a ½-inch grinder plate into a large dish. M added just enough broth from the pot to make a soft batter, discarding the rest. Q then returned the mixture to the pot and added 1 bulb of garlic, 2 cups of chopped onion, 2 tablespoons of pepper, and 2 tablespoons of salt. Once the mixture had come to a boil, I removed it from the stove and poured it into four glass molds. K covered each of the molds with cloth and a plate, placing large stones on top to make a press. The next morning, M turned the molds upside down. Q shaved off four thin slices and set them on the table for breakfast, but I was already in the basement, fetching another head.

The Rules

I called the meeting to order and asked for a motion to approve the minutes of the previous meeting. K moved to approve. M seconded the motion. Any amendments to the minutes, I asked. Q rose and stated that the minutes indicated I was present at the last meeting, when in fact I had been absent. I looked at K. K was looking at M. If the minutes say I was there, K said, then I must have been there. No, said Q. The minutes are incorrect. M agreed. Q sat down. I was not there, M said. There is an error in the minutes. Q nodded. But K persisted. I was there, in the same chair as always, at the head of the table, just like now. K pointed. I gave M a severe look. M looked at Q. Q was playing chess on a hand-held device. Perhaps there has been a mistake, M said. The minutes are not always accurate. K agreed. Language is very imprecise. I nodded, and rose. And if it has been agreed — as previous minutes indicate — that there is a gap between the signifier and the signified, an *aporia* over which various ideologies and discursive practices compete for hegemony, then the notion of *verification*, the very essence of the Law itself, becomes highly fraught. M frowned. I asked Q if this was not the case. Q moved from A4 to D3, capturing a pawn. There is a motion on the table, K said. All in favour, I said. K and M nodded. The motion passed with one abstention. I made a note of it in the minutes, and called for the Officer and Committee Reports.

Un Chien *Andalou*

K divided the superior rectus midway between its origin and its point of insertion. M suggested that removing some of the fat might bring the optic nerve more fully into view. Q concurred. I observed that at the posterior part of the orbit, three structures were crossing the nerve: the naso-ciliary nerve, the ophthalmic artery, and the superior ophthalmic vein. K carefully cleaned all three and followed out the branches before disengaging the delicate, thread-like short ciliary nerves from the fat surrounding the optic nerve. M selected the strongest member of the short ciliary group and followed it backwards to the ciliary ganglion, a minute body situated on the lateral side of the optic nerve in the posterior part of the orbit. With patience and care, Q isolated the communicating branches which the naso-ciliary nerve and the inferior division of the oculo-motor nerve give to the ciliary ganglion. Now the sympathetic branch from the internal carotid plexus was appararent. I cleared away the adipose tissue which lay lateral to the ganglion and secured the abducent nerve which entered the surface of the lateral rectus. Then K, M and Q carefully cleaned the optic nerve. Once all the structures had been found and cleaned, I studied them in detail.

A Test

M

Q K

I E F

P T O Z

L P E D P

E C F D E D

F C Z P F E L

Timewarp

Q used the 60x pocket loupe to check the trichomes. The heads were approximately 25 percent amber. K said that was perfect and would give a nice cerebral effect. Q preferred a body high and told K to wait. Another week would allow the CBD and CBN levels to increase, Q said. M said that if Q wanted couch weed then an indica would have been a better choice. I suggested indica for next season and passed around the trimmers. K and I cut the plants at the base of the stalks. M and Q removed the larger fan leaves to prevent mold. Q and I trimmed off the damaged leaves and buds. Then K and M tied the plants upside down in the drying shed. I suggested cutting a few buds for the dehydrator so there was something to smoke while the rest was drying. K said the bud would taste like shit. M and Q said do it anyway. After ten days Q bent the central stem on the one of the larger floral clusters. The stem snapped briskly. That was a good sign, I said. K, M and I collected the plants for trimming, careful not to shake or damage the calyxes. Q spread a tarp out over the floor and set chairs in each corner. Working up from the bottom of each plant, all the leaves, stems and popcorn buds were trimmed and tossed into the middle of the tarp, while the larger buds were placed in empty beer flats with holes poked through the bottom. Then the buds were trimmed, working up from the bottom again, while rotating counter-clockwise. When all the buds were trimmed, K brought out a box of Mason jars for curing. K and I filled each jar with bud. M counted 64 jars. Q said a celebration was in order and brought out the Roor, but I was already busy collecting the schwag, which I knew would make some fine bubble hash.

K

Fine Bubble Hash

I brought the paint mixer, K brought the bucket, M brought ice and water, and Q brought the 20-gallon four-bag bubble hash kit. Q placed the bags in the bucket, beginning with the 25μ screen bag, followed by the 73μ, the 160μ, and the 220μ. M filled the bucket with the ice and the water, being sure to raise the water above the level of the screen to prevent contaminants from entering the first few bags. K took the trim out of the freezer and poured it into the bag. I thought there was room for more ice and emptied four more trays into the bag. It's all in the ice, Q said. K stirred the mixture on high for 16 minutes to make sure all the frozen trichomes separated from the plant material. Then the mixture was left to sit for half an hour to allow the gland heads to settle. Q put on Datsik and lit a joint. When the 220μ bag had settled, I removed it, being careful to not let any pieces of leaf into the bags underneath. M wanted to squeeze it, but K said that might force contaminants into the extract. Q removed the next bag, letting the water drain into the bucket, and observed the screen. There was a decent amount of dark, lower-grade resin. I scraped the screen gently with silicon spatula and set the collected material on the pressing screen. The 73μ bag took a while to drain, so K stretched it over a bowl, which made collecting the resin easier. I looked at the extract and noticed it was light-colored and highly fragrant. M was careful to rinse the bags back into the bucket so as not to waste any gland heads. Finally I took the 25μ bag out and squeezed it hard to remove all the liquid. The resin on this screen was white. The Philosopher's Stone, Q said. M suggested sampling the product immediately, but I knew this higher-quality resin still needed to be pressed in order to ensure proper drying.

It's *All* In the *Game*

K was driving, M and Q were in the backseat, I was riding shotgun. K pulled the vehicle up to the end of the driveway. Turn right, I said. K accelerated onto the road and turned right. Stop at the intersection, M said. K brought the vehicle to a full stop. Which way, asked K. Turn right, Q said. K complied. When the vehicle had reached the posted speed limit, K checked the rearview mirror. M was looking out the window. Q was looking at K. I told K to watch the road. M asked how much longer. K and I looked at the clock on the dashboard. The clock said 10:15. I told M there were still 46 blocks to go. Q asked if there was any music. K said check the glove box. I opened the glove box and took out The Four Tops' *16 Greatest Hits*. Play track 15, K said. I inserted the disc and entered 15. The music started to play. Increase the volume M said. Just as I reached for the volume control, K stopped the vehicle at an intersection. There were three other vehicles sitting at each corner. Which way, K asked. Turn right, M said. K activated the appropriate turn signal indicator. None of the other vehicles moved. I told K to indicate to the vehicle coming in the opposite direction that it should proceed. K rolled down the window and signaled. The vehicle pulled forward and turned right. Then the other two vehicles advanced through the intersection. When the intersection was clear, K pulled forward and turned right. The song was still playing on the stereo. K, M and Q sang along. The vehicle gained speed. This is going to be quite an adventure, M said. K and Q nodded, but I knew that without a map, a destination, and only one CD, this trip would quickly become tedious.

Theory of Prose

M was writing a paragraph. Q told M to begin with the topic sentence. The topic sentence should be the most general statement in the paragraph but should also be specific enough to express the main point, I said. M nodded. K added that a good topic sentence should also indicate which of the Eight Modes it will be using: Description, Process, Comparison and Contrast, Analogy, Cause and Effect, Classification and Division, Definition, or Narrative. M asked for examples. Ants are so much like human beings as to be an embarrassment, I said. Analogy, M said. Correct, K said. Like the game itself, a baseball is composed of many layers, Q said. Classification, M said. No, division, I said. Classification is the grouping of items into categories; division takes a single object or concept and divides it into parts. M nodded. Reification is so characteristic of market society that many people have forgotten what the word actually means, I said. Definition, M said. Excellent, Q said. What about narrative paragraphs, M asked. Q looked at K. K shrugged. Those are different, I said. In a narrative paragraph the topic is left unstated, and the reader needs to infer one from the details. What if the reader fails to infer the correct topic, M asked. That never happens, I said.

The Plot

Q secured a digital watch as a timer, I secured stabilizers that looked like cotton wool balls, K secured the mercury fulminate crystals. M secured the other ingredients: glycerin, nitrate, sulfuric acid, nitrobenzene, silver azide, and liquid acetone. The device was to be set on an airliner bound for the United States, with stopovers in East and Southeast Asia. Q put two 9-volt batteries in each device, as a power source. I connected the batteries to the light bulb filaments that would act as detonators. K and M wired an SCR as the switch to trigger the filaments. Getting the device onto the plane was easy. There was an external socket hidden under the watch base where the wires were pushed, an alteration so small that Q could still wear the watch in a normal manner. M got the batteries past airport security by concealing them in the hollowed-out heels of a pair of boots. K and I smuggled the nitroglycerin on board inside bottles of contact lens solution. Q planted the device inside a life jacket under a seat, and disembarked. M, K and I then boarded more flights and repeated the procedure. After all the devices were planted, Q, M, K and I boarded planes to Pakistan. I financed the plot via a front organization.

Umbrella

I brought in a new piece to be workshopped. K asked if the piece was a segment from a longer manuscript, or if it was supposed to stand alone. I replied both. This piece is part of a longer work and is also intended to be read on its own, I said. M thought that the piece needed some work. K agreed. The characterization was weak, there was no sense of conflict or suspense, and the narrative point of view was cold. Why should a reader care about these characters, M asked. Q added that the plot was static, and suggested I perform a plot analysis to get a better sense of how the narrative was progressing. K agreed. Narratives have a setting, a conflict, rising action, and a crisis, followed by *dénouement* and a resolution, though some writers don't like closure, preferring instead the poetics of the open text, K said. M added that if I was after was a micro-fiction, I needed a central prop: a sharp, resonant image for the reader to focus on, like an umbrella. Put in an umbrella, Q said. I was silent. K laughed and looked at M. I wrote the word at the top of the manuscript. Q asked if anyone else had comments. K suggested we move on to the next piece, a scene from an existential novel about four characters on a road trip through Death Valley. I nodded and pretended to take notes, but really I was wondering if this piece would have been better with seventeen rather than eighteen sentences.

From 'Through the Valley'

K rolled out the tent. Q and M took the corners on one side, K and I took the other. Q and M started shaking the tent vigorously. K and I did the same. Then I removed the poles from the bag. K took the first pole and tried to thread it through the hoops, but the fabric caught and the pole disassembled. M and Q were also threading a pole from the other side, causing the tent to pull in different directions. I told M and Q to wait until K had the first pole through the hoops. K frowned. Q fiddled with the pole. Once the first pole was through, I fastened the grommet and bent the pole to form an arc. K tried to fasten the grommet on the opposite side, but the fabric didn't reach. I told K to hold on because the fabric had caught half way down the pole, but K didn't listen. M laughed at K. Q was bending a pole. I went to the side K was on and fastened the grommet. One pole was in place. Q told K to help guide the second pole through the hoop. When K pulled, the pole came apart and the arc flipped on its side. M was hammering stakes into the ground and attaching bungee cords. I reassembled the second pole while Q and K worked on the grommets. Then the tent tilted. M was attaching a bungee cord to a yucca. K told M to wait, the tent wasn't stable. The bungee cords should go on last. Q and I steadied the tent while K and M unrolled the fly. Once the fly was in place, M, Q, K and I hammered in pegs and attached the lines. The tent was done. I climbed inside, and bid K, M, and Q goodnight.

Sic Semper Tyrannis

M arrived at the Curia to sit at the head of the forum. As usual, K, Q and I took seats around the tyrant. I was the first to petition M, with a request for a pardon for an exiled brother. I knew that M would refuse the request, and that this would give K, Q and I occasion to surround M to make appeals. As M rose, I grabbed the cuff of the purple tunic, which was the signal to begin the attack. K was positioned behind M, and was the first to stab the dictator, landing a dagger just above the collarbone. M turned and asked K what is this violence. As Q approached, dagger in hand, K stabbed M in the arm with a stylus. Q and I then joined the attack. I struck M with a second blow deep in the chest. K stabbed fervently, accidentally cutting Q. Covered in blood, M tried to cover up for posterity, pulling at the edges of the tattered toga. In the end, M was stabbed 64 times before collapsing upon a statue of Melpomene. Later it was reported that in the final moments of the attack M had used the expression *Kai su, teknon*, but I heard no such utterance, merely a groan.

Art as Technique

Q administered a high-frequency electric shock that rendered the pig unconscious. Then I hoisted it onto an overhead rail for slaughter. K cut the carotid artery and jugular vein to drain the blood and to relax the muscles, which would make for easier dehairing. The pig was left hanging for about twelve minutes while M collected the blood in a barrel. Q operated the machine that dropped the pig into a tub of scalding water to loosen up the hair. I rotated to insure uniform scalding. K moved the animal to another machine equipped with metal-tipped beaters that scoured the skin. M removed the remaining hairs by singeing the carcass with a gas flame. After sticking, bleeding and scalding, Q severed the head from the backbone at the atlas joint, continuing the cut down through the windpipe and esophagus. I inspected the head and cut out the tongue. K applied the inspection stamp. Then it was time to gut the animal. M separated the hams. Q split the sternum. I opened the ventral side down the entire length of the carcass. K removed the abdominal organs into the gut pan. M and Q separated the edible from the non-edible parts. I harvested the intestines. Finally, K split the carcass in half and applied a salt solution to remove the blood, feces, and bits of hair and bone. At this stage, K, M and Q thought that the process was complete, but I knew that a chilling period was still required before the animal would be cut into even smaller pieces and prepared for packaging and shipping.

Against Expression

I sourced, K weighed, M cleaned, and Q processed the raw material. After an hour or so in a pressure cooker, the mash was transferred to a sterilized steel vat to cool. Then K stirred in a teaspoon of yeast. M asked if the mixture could be consumed now, but Q explained that it had to sit for about twelve days. After this fermentation period was complete, the process of separating substances according to their volatility would begin, Q said. In the meantime, I procured all the components needed to construct a distillation apparatus: a 16-litre beaker, a 4-litre beaker, two rubber stoppers, one foot of coiled copper tubing, a condensing jacket, a thermometer, and a bucket of crushed ice. K placed a stopper in the large beaker. M attached the coil to the stopper. Q fitted the condensing jacket around the coil. I filled the jacket with crushed ice and water. Next, K put a second rubber stopper with a hole for tubing into the smaller beaker. M attached the other end of the tubing. When the still was assembled, Q placed the large beaker on the element and the small beaker on the counter. I heated the mash in the large beaker to 192 degrees, the exact temperature at which the desired substance would separate. Once the essence had passed through the cooling coil, condensed, and dropped down into the second beaker, K declared that the distillate was ready to be consumed. M and Q nodded, but I knew that if the goal was a completely clear and tasteless product, this procedure would have to be repeated 63 times, until all traces of the originary substance had been removed.

The Rules

K rose to present the Officer's Report. The slaughtering and processing of the pig went off without any problems, K said. A document titled "Art as Technique" was passed around the table. M, Q and I read the document while K turned on the projector. The video showed a pig flapping about on the floor before being clubbed unconscious, kicked, and thrown onto a conveyer belt. In the next scene, the neck was cut and the animal was stuck onto a hook, while blood drained into a dirty steel vat. The carcass then was burnt, skinned, and decapitated. K paused the video and asked if there were any questions or comments. Q wanted to know if that was the end of the video. No said, K. The next scene shows the carcass being separated into edible and non-edible parts. That will be enough, M said. Fine, K said. Please note, however, that in the future, a chilling period will be required before the meat can be prepared for final processing, packaging and shipping. This allows the flesh to firm up. I nodded. K sat down. Any further discussion, I asked. There was no discussion. Motion to accept the report. Q moved from H7 to G4. So moved, said M. All in favour. K, M, and Q nodded. It's unanimous, I said.

In the Eye of the Storm

M told Q, K and I to begin the gybe. Q brought the *Cardinal* up full-face against the hurricane. The first gust put the guardrail under and the lower spreaders touched the water. K winched the storm jib hard. I helped put the helm down again and waited to see what would happen. The mast slowly regained an upright position and the boat began to move windward, up over the apex of a wave then down the fifty-foot slope into the next trough. Q was just climbing into the cockpit when another wave hit, knocking the vessel down beyond 90 degrees. M struggled to stay in the boat. A spinnaker pole burst its lashings. The head car fitting at the top of the mainsail had broken, and both the mainsail and the number two, which were lashed to the deck, were ripped. I decided not to venture beyond the jigger mast. A half an hour later the wind had lost its edge. K thought the worst of it had passed, but Q said that was only round one, there were still many miles to go. The wind was down to 35 knots and I knew more sail was needed. K checked the deck and stowed the torn number two. Q set to work repairing the mainsail, drilling holes for the needle to save time. M wanted to rest, but I knew there was no time for that. The conditions had changed, and a new strategy was needed, so I set about charting a course.

Breaking the Law

Q claimed that K had ordered the Code Red because I had told K to do so. Objection, M said. And when things went bad I had cut K loose. M objected again. The judge said that would be all, but Q pressed further. According to Q, I had ordered a subordinate to sign a phony transfer order. Objection, M shouted. And then I had doctored the log books. M tuned to Q and said damn it Q that's enough. Q demanded the truth a fourth time: Did I order — but I interrupted. I asked if Q wanted answers. Q said that was an entitlement. Did Q want answers, I asked again, louder. Q wanted the truth. Q can't handle the truth, I said. There was silence in the court. Then I began: People live in a world with walls, and those walls have to be guarded by men with guns, I said. Who's going to do that? M? K? Q? I had a greater responsibility than Q could possibly fathom. Q wept for Santiago and cursed the marines. Q had that luxury. Q had the luxury of not knowing what I knew: That Santiago's death, while tragic, probably saved lives. Words like honor, code, loyalty . . . these words were the backbone to a life spent defending something, I said. But Q used them as a punch line. So I had neither the time nor the inclination to explain things to Q, and I didn't give a damn what Q was entitled to. Q remained unmoved: did I order the Code Red? There was a job that had to be done and I had done it, I said. Did I order the Code Red, Q demanded. Goddamn right, I said.

Thanks for Looking

I was too busy at work to finish this project: a '92 Mazda B2600i Ext cab 2WD with an '82 Mercedes OM617 3.0L 5-cyl turbo diesel swapped in. K said the new engine was awesome, except for the head gasket which had a small leak. M piped the 4-inch chrome stack off the turbo which sounded sick, exactly like a big rig. Q mated the engine up to the Mazda 5-speed tranny, making part swaps simple. I dropped the chassis about 4 inches, giving the vehicle a nice stance. K added the 16-inch AR chromies. I had wanted to put some bigger Chevy rims on, but was too busy working to do that. M installed a custom hidden hitch welded in between the rear frame rails coming out behind the license plate so it wouldn't hit the ground. Q put in the propane injection which added about another 16–20HP. I pimped the interior with Bauhn 4-inch rounds in the back, separate tweets on top of the dash, new red carpet and sweet black Honda Prelude buckets. I thought the box could also use some love — the roll pan was a bit rusty and had a few dents in it, but never got to that. Also the valance for the wipers got bent when K took them off, so that needs to be replaced. I put lots of work went into this vehicle to make it durable, stylish, fun, and efficient — now it needs someone else to finish it off.

Reader Response

K was a character with a back-story: a well-kept, hard-working, Kafkaesque study in contrasts. K was like kryptonite: impossible to crack. Quick-witted, skeptical, and lucky-in-love, by the end of the story K had become just another broken-down stock character trying to click with the kids. In contrast, M was more mysterious, an esteemed, determined, and unkempt *poet maudite*, malnourished and emaciated, but also a motivated academic composing an MA on grammar at MIT, under the mentorship of Dr. Noam Chomsky himself. And then there was Q. Similar to K, Q had unique qualities and was also trying to pique the curiosity of the clique, except that Q was quite a well-torqued character. Q was on some kind of quest, but became quarrelsome, awkward, and quirky as the story progressed. In one scene, Q became quick-tempered in a queue to meet the Queen. And whenever I entered the room, Q would squint and squirm. In fact, it seemed I exerted this indescribable influence on every individual in each and every instance.

Lovin' It

M set the timer and flipped the patties onto the grill. Q hit the sear beeper, I put the buns in the oven, and K set the timer. M flipped the patties. Q took the reconstituted onions out of a bowl and dropped them on the meat: t-con, t-con, t-con, t-con. I heard the bun oven beep so I opened the door and took out the crowns. K lined the crowns up in a row and gave each one a squirt of mustard and a squirt of ketchup. The dispenser was pre-measured for ten-in-ones and for quarter-pounders — K correctly chose quarter-pounders. Now it was time to place the pickles. M put two pickles on each crown. Q noticed that the pickles on the third crown were smaller than the others. K agreed and said three pickles would be OK in this case. I took another regular-sized pickle and placed it on the third crown. Q nodded. When I was done M placed the lettuce. K asked for a cheese count. Cheese for four, Q said. Suddenly the sear beeper went off: *beep-beep-beep, beep-beep-beep, beep-beep-beep.* M took the patties off the grill and slid them on the crowns. K scooped the heels off the top shelf of the bun warmer, pushing the tray out from underneath so they landed on each burger, right on top of the t-cons. M stopped the timer: 67 seconds. Good time, Q said. M and K agreed. I nodded, but I couldn't help but wonder if adding that third pickle wasn't responsible for those three extra seconds.

Rising Action

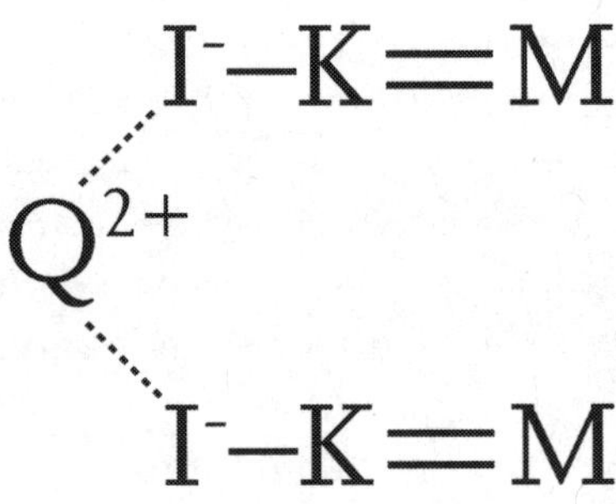

M

The *Avant-Garde* Never Gives Up

I had writer's block. K said there was no such thing as writer's block and that the problem I had was a big ego. M agreed. Century after century of Private Citizen speaking to Public World has become tiresome, Q said. The liberal, neo-Habermasian notion of a public world was a con, K said, never mind the epistemological dilemmas associated with the valorization of the private individual. Or the citizen, M added. What does that mean, I said. Try procedural writing, Q said. Take a newspaper and a pair of scissors. Choose an article as long as the intended poem and cut out the article. Then cut out each of the words that make up the article and put them in a bag. Shake it gently. Then take out the scraps one after the other in the order in which they left the bag. Copy conscientiously. By following this procedure carefully, Q said, I would be a writer, infinitely original and endowed with a sensibility that was charming though beyond the understanding of the vulgar. That's already been done, M said. Then write a story without using the letter E. Done. Take an existing text like *Paradise Lost*, and cross parts out, Q said. Done, M said. Use the Fibonacci sequence as a compositional device. Done. Alphabetize responses to the Rorschach inkblot test. Done. Done, done, done, M said. What about a story without the letter I, Q said. K looked at M. Impossible, I said.

Epimythium

K made a false accusation against M, demanding that M return a loaf of bread which K alleged M had borrowed. When M denied the claim, K summoned Q as a witness. Sharing certain characteristics with K, Q was compelled to testify that M didn't owe just one loaf of bread, but four. Based on this questionable testimony, M was sentenced to return four loaves of bread to K. Sometime later, M and Q were found dead in a ditch. While it is customary to induce from this narrative a moral lesson — "wicked liars get their just desserts" — I read it more pragmatically, *i.e.*, as an *instruction manual*.

P.O.V.

M was wearing a tight green velour track suit with nothing underneath. Q and K were wearing red shirts and black ball caps. I was working the camera. K and Q came to the door with a pizza box. M opened the door and took the pizza. K said the total was $20, but M had no money. Q said no problem, personal assets were fine. K nodded and smiled. M said Oh ya and backed inside as Q and K followed. I cut the scene to move to the kitchen. In the next scene, M swayed topless while Q and K jacked off. Then K got closer and unzipped M from behind. M curled a finger at Q. Q bent M over the table. K kneeled behind Q. I zoomed in on fingers gripping an ass. M squirmed as K took over. K was licking M on the inner thigh, while Q slathered on the oil. I took the camera off the tripod for some hand-held action. Q lay on the floor with M crouched above, sliding back and forth. K drew M up and pressed in hard. I tried to get K, M and Q all at once with a canted angle shot but the kitchen island was in the way. I saw an ass grinding back and forth: Q was inside M. K had erect nipples. I tried to move the island to get in closer but I didn't want to interrupt the scene, so I put the camera on the floor. M saw what I was doing, and picked up the camera. Suddenly, I was in the scene. M returned and bent Q over, thrusting hard. I spread to let M in. K and Q were kissing. Q was naked. M was wearing the red cap K had on. I couldn't tell K from M or Q, but I didn't care — I knew exactly what was coming next.

Cathedral

Q brought the yellow candle and matches, I brought the cinnamon, K brought the paper and crayons, M brought the glass of water. Q began the spell by taking a sip of the water. Feel the liquid going down, K said. Q looked at K and nodded. Now imagine a circle of light, I said. Q concentrated. K said that in order for the spell to work, the eyes had to be closed. M was watching closely to make sure Q followed the instructions. Now with open eyes light the yellow candle, M said. Q struck a match and lit the candle. I began the spell. Muse Goddess, spirit of all things, be here now, to guide and to teach, and to help Q to find inspiration in this world. M told Q to look around and to take note of any shadows, reflections or light. Look for textures and colors, M said. Taste the water, and enjoy the feeling. Sprinkle some cinnamon in the air. Breathe the air. Notice the smells. Q sniffed the air and looked around. K continued. Muse Goddess, Q is not always observant, and forgets to treasure the gifts of the Goddess. Q gets stuck in the ordinary world, and doesn't look beyond. Goddess, help Q to grow past that. K looked at Q. Q nodded. Sometimes Q misuses the gifts of the Muse, M said, locking away real talent because of a fear of failing. The Muse provides inspiration, but Q is too scared to try. Everything Q does is filtered through a harsh self-critic that judges everything based on the standards of others. Q forgets that all creativity is sacred. When M was done I told Q to take the paper and crayons and to draw something symbolizing creativity. Maybe a flower, K said. Or the moon, M said. The crayon represents the freedom of the child to create a world, I said. Do not judge this work, Q — simply draw, as a child would, demanding nothing. Revel in the act of creation itself. Q put the crayon to the paper and drew a square. Keep going, K said. Q continued. Soon the square became a cube. Then Q attached the cube to other cubes, each with its own elaborate internal structure. Q was in a trance. What is that, K asked. It's some kind of diagram, M said. Or maybe a blueprint. K thought it was a map. But as I looked closer, it became clear what Q had made. Thanks to the Muse for this gift, I said.

The Raw and the Cooked

I removed the surface materials, dismantled the framework, then passed the supports to K. M removed the entry points, which had been installed in a more or less explicit manner. Q suggested that certain elements might be retained in order to create something new out of the remnants of the old, but K, M and I agreed that the task here was to destroy all the old machinery to which the elements belonged, and of which they themselves were pieces. Q nodded and began to dismantle the balances one at a time, using an instrument I had never seen before. Meanwhile, K separated the exterior from the interior of the structure, a step made easier by the fact that the privileged place-ethnology of the entire edifice had been compromised from the very beginning. M reciprocated by knocking out the posts that gave the structure its structurality, but which escaped structurality themselves. At this juncture, Q wanted to know where and how this notion of a structurality-outside-structure arose, but already I had unhinged the opposition between the sensible and the intelligible, and was on to disassembling its several components.

Storytime

K told M that Q was a little bunny that wanted to run away. M said that I, the mother bunny, wouldn't like that. If Q runs away, M said, I will run after Q. But what if Q became a fish in a trout stream, and swam away, K asked. If Q became a fish in a trout stream, M said, I would become a fisherman, and I would fish for Q. If I became a fisherman, K said, Q could become a rock high on the mountain. If Q became a rock high on the mountain, M said, I would become a mountain climber and climb to Q. If I became a mountain climber, K replied, Q could become a crocus in a hidden garden. If Q became a crocus in a hidden garden, M said, I would become a gardener, and I would find Q. If I became a gardener, K continued, Q could become a bird, and fly away. If Q became a bird and flew away, M replied, I would become a tree that Q came home to. If I became a tree, K said, Q could become a little sailboat, and sail away. If Q turned in to a little sailboat, M said, I would become the wind and would blow the boat where I wanted it to go. If I became the wind, K said, Q could join a circus and fly away on a flying trapeze. If Q went flying on a flying trapeze, said M, I would become a tightrope walker and I would walk across the air to Q. If I became a tightrope walker walking across the air, K said, then Q will become a little boy and run into a house. If Q becomes a little boy running into a house, M said, then I will become a mother and will catch and hug the little boy. Shucks, said K. Q may as well stay put. And so Q did. Have a carrot, I said.

The Rules

M had a report. A sub-committee met to investigate and clarify four points of grammar and style that were causing confusion in the minutes, M said. The first has to do with collective pronoun agreement, the second with passive and active voice, the third with commas and restrictive clauses, and the fourth with correct usage of the first-person singular. I looked at the clock. The clock said 10:15AM. Q rose and went to the board. Is this sentence correct: "The sub-committee presented their report." That is not correct, M said. I made a note in the minutes that the sub-committee did not present their report. M continued. Collective nouns such as "sub-committee" identify a class or set, and ordinarily a set functions as a single unit. The correct expression is "The sub-committee presented its report." Q nodded. I corrected the minutes. K rose. Did the subcommittee put its signature on the report? M looked at K. K looked at Q. Q moved from E4 to C7. That is not correct, said M. When the elements which compose a set act as individuals, then the collective pronoun is used. The correct sentence is "The subcommittee put their signatures on the report." I made a note in the minutes. Q looked up. How many members are on the sub-committee, K asked. One, I said.

Bend It Like Q

Q began in a largely defensive role, stepping forward for the first free kick, but K took it instead and banged it into the wall. The first significant contribution Q made was in the 12th minute: a long pass that curled around M, although K quickly lost possession. In the 24th minute, Q stole the ball from M and sent K forward to a goal. But just minutes later I intercepted a pass from K and scored from within the area as Q and K looked on. Q took a free kick in the 48th minute from the right side, near the sideline — a perfect position for that famous left foot — but the kick was headed away by M. A minute later M came across to take a corner from the left, but I easily handled that low attempt. In the second half K tapped in a nice cross from Q while M and I waited for an offside call that never came. Q took another corner from the left and got the ball to K, but K volleyed high. Four minutes later I dribbled past Q on a counter-attack and chipped the ball into the net. K got a corner kick, passing a short ball to Q. Q lobbed the ball quickly on the net, but I had no trouble handling that attempt in front of the post. When Q came on strong in the 64th minute by capitalizing on a bouncing ball with a quick header to tie the game, the crowd broke into song. Q ran to the wall, K punched the air, and M looked down, but I knew this was just the beginning of a long and bitter contest for position.

Irony

I heated the end of a quarter-inch iron rod to a bright cherry red. K took the rod and held it at a 32-degree angle flush with the far edge of the anvil face. M tapered the point. Q shifted the rod to the near edge of the anvil and held it level in order to draw out the correct length and thickness. When Q was done, I tested the shank by inserting it into the smaller hole of the header. The shank fits, I said. Next, K placed the rod over the edge of the hardie, about half an inch above the top of the drawn-out shank. M hammered on the rod just hard enough to cut it only partway through. Q inserted the shank into a small hole on the upper face of the header and twisted the rod back and forth to break it off cleanly at the point where it had been scored. Then I placed the header on the anvil with the point in the pritchel hole. K used a ball peen hammer to upset the head. M quenched the spike in water, header and all. Finally, Q tapped the spike loose and held it up for inspection. Excellent, K said. Nice and straight, M said. Perfect length, Q said. Now for the wooden cross, I said.

The Medium Is the Message

K placed the transformer on the circuit board, making sure to leave a space for the oscillator. M inserted the leads of the oscillator, placing it far to the right. Q said the copper side of the board should face down, with the oscillator on the side without copper. M followed the instructions. As K was more dexterous than I, I told K to bend the leads of the oscillator onto the board. K was just about to solder the pins of the oscillator to the copper foil when M told K to slow down. Too much solder could create bridges between parts that are not supposed to be connected, M said. When K was done, Q stripped one end of the red wire and inserted it into the bottom left hole on the circuit board. I took the red wire from the battery clip and inserted that into another hole that was connected by copper foil to the first hole. M inserted the white transformer wire into a hole that was connected to the upper left pin of the oscillator and soldered the wire to the copper foil. I cut one of the clip leads in half and gave it to K. K attached alligator clips to each piece and handed them to M. M stripped the insulation from the last half inch of each piece and gave them to Q. Then Q inserted the black wire from the battery clip into a hole connected to the lower right pin of the oscillator. I inserted the stripped end of one of the alligator clip leads into a hole that was also connected to the lower right pin of the oscillator. K joined the two wires to the copper foil. M inserted the stripped end of the other alligator clip into a hole that was connected to the top right pin of the oscillator and soldered the wire to the copper foil. This will be the antenna connector, M said. Is the transmitter operational, M asked. I looked at Q. First open the phone plug, and insert the blue and green wires from the transformer into the plastic handle, Q said. Put one of the transformer wires into one hole and solder it, then put the other wire into the other hole and solder that. M complied. When the metal has cooled, screw the handle back onto the metal phone plug. Then the transmitter will be functional. Once these final steps were completed, M, K and Q wanted to broadcast a message immediately. I was doubtful, however, that this transmission would ever have any meaningful content.

A Perfect Plan

M used a number of carefully placed pylons to divert the armoured vehicle into a collision. All transmissions in the area were blocked after Q planted high-power phone and radio jammers in the trunk of a car, rendering the armoured vehicle unable to report the delay. Meanwhile, K, posing as a temp, released 8oz of Liquid Ass into the bank's ventilation system, flooding the building with a rancid odour. At exactly 10:00AM, fifteen minutes before the scheduled arrival of the armoured vehicle, Q and I pulled up in an air-conditioning repair company van and gained access to the holdings area through the ventilation ducts. K neutralized the security guard monitoring the surveillance system. Once inside the central holdings room, I executed and disarmed the guards while Q bagged the money that had been prepared for collection. K sounded the fire alarm, automatically unlocking the fire exit doors and signaling M to bring the get away van to the side of the garage. A series of explosives were detonated around the bank opening a path to an escape route that led to a parking lot. Once the van arrived at the lot, the gang was supposed to split up the money and depart in separate vehicles, but I had another plan.

A Little Lesson

Q drew a horizontal red line across the board and told K to solve the problem. K went to the board and used the line Q had drawn as the base of a triangle. That was wrong. Q told K to sit down. I was called to correct the error K had made. I looked at K. K looked at M. Q turned to the board and drew a vertical green line underneath the red triangle. Q pointed at the green line. I went to the board and drew a circle around the line Q had drawn. Q pointed at the green circle and looked at K. I sat down. Q used a ruler to measure the line through the green circle. The line was 8½ inches long. Q asked M if the base of the red triangle K had drawn was equal to the diameter of the green circle I drew. M went to the board and used the ruler to measure the base of the red triangle. The base was 5½ inches wide. M told Q that the lines were not equal. Q told M to sit down and looked at K. The lesson was over. Later, K told M that I had solved the problem, but I knew it was Q.

Universal Grammar

I was it. K ran behind the hedge, M climbed onto the deck, Q ran around the perimeter of the yard. I went after M because there was only one way onto the deck and M would have no escape. M saw I was coming and tried to climb onto the railing. Q told M to get down from there. M jumped down and ran behind the barbeque, pushing a deck chair forward as a barricade. I dodged the chair and ran along the sliding door to the left of the barbeque. I tagged M. M was it. I ran off the deck towards K. M came down the stairs. Q was still running in a circle around the yard. Q was half the age of K, M and I and didn't seem to understand how to play this game. M stood in the middle of the yard watching Q. Then M stepped forward and tagged Q as Q ran by. Q was it. Q stopped and tagged M back then ran under the deck. M was it again. M turned towards K and I. K ran out from behind the hedge toward the old cherry tree. M was in pursuit. K reached the tree and stepped on to a rung that had been nailed midway up the trunk. When M reached the tree K was swinging on a branch. M tagged K. K was it. M jumped down and ran under the deck with Q. I was behind the hedge. K sat in the tree picking cherries. Q came out from under the deck and asked if the game was still on. K said no. M and Q wanted to play some more, but as the light in the yard faded, I knew this game was coming to its end.

Mutual *Aid*

K was in prison. I gained entrance to the prison under the pretense of delivering a gift. Inside the watch was a small piece of paper upon which the plan had been written in a tiny cipher. Outside, M and Q were already in position. At exactly 10:15AM, K entered the yard in a green flannel dressing-gown, which was the signal for M to draw the carriage near the gate. K moved to the edge of the yard, shuffled along the footpath, then checked the location of the sentry. When M signaled that the carriage path was clear, K flung off the green dressing-gown in two quick movements and started to run. Two peasants piling wood at the other end of the yard shouted stop, alarming the sentry. M pulled the carriage up to the gate just as K came running through. Q opened the carriage door. K jumped into the carriage. M said gallop. The carriage took off down the street, turning sharply into a narrow lane, past the same wall of the yard where the peasants had been piling wood. In just a few minutes, K, M, and Q reached the Nevsky Prospect, and alighted into a house on a side street, where I was waiting with a pair of scissors.

Ludibrium

M	V	I	L	I	A	R	Q	Z	W	P	Q	O	A	B	D
W	L	Y	E	I	M	A	L	Y	V	R	E	F	L	J	N
Z	G	O	Z	X	G	C	Z	K	Z	R	O	H	J	W	M
R	K	N	Y	E	Y	O	X	B	V	G	B	Y	W	T	J
F	L	V	Z	J	N	E	M	P	J	I	U	P	G	G	H
X	T	B	A	B	H	N	O	R	O	I	T	W	S	H	G
N	Z	C	K	D	L	S	G	O	D	N	J	J	S	C	W
P	M	X	G	E	U	I	X	H	I	L	W	J	M	O	T
A	F	S	Q	Y	Z	R	K	B	A	S	E	I	M	C	Q
R	P	U	R	L	C	Q	F	I	K	M	S	V	J	S	G
Q	E	I	L	I	H	V	B	X	J	J	R	P	I	T	S
K	F	E	Z	Q	M	K	I	Y	U	G	V	C	Y	U	Z
K	H	T	A	R	Y	C	S	M	P	U	K	Q	H	O	C
W	J	A	I	N	E	H	F	G	Q	T	V	U	W	Z	U
S	X	Y	U	I	Q	L	H	J	E	E	M	X	A	C	W
R	V	O	K	H	S	K	K	Y	Q	S	B	I	X	Q	F

Something for Everyone

Q put oil in a heavy-bottomed pan over medium heat. When the oil was hot, I added the onions, the carrot, and the celery. K seasoned with salt and pepper. M sautéed for 2 minutes. Q added the tomato and garlic. Two minutes later, I added the white beans. K stirred in the water while M added the rosemary and seasoned with more salt and pepper. The liquid was brought to a boil. Q reduced the heat to medium-low and continued to cook until the beans were tender, about 1¼ to 1½ hours. Meanwhile, I combined the remaining olive oil, rosemary and garlic in a small saucepan. K brought the mixture to a simmer and cooked until the garlic was golden, about 10 to 12 minutes. M removed the saucepan from the heat and strained, discarding the rosemary and garlic. Using a hand-held blender, Q pureed half of the soup. I added more salt and pepper. Then K stirred in the cooked pasta and continued to simmer for 15 minutes. M removed the soup from the heat. Q ladled into individual bowls. I divided the bread. This recipe yielded 4 equal servings.

Q

Limited Omniscience

I slipped on the noose and kicked out the stool. K and M heard a thud and ran upstairs. K gasped. The beam had broken and I was on the floor. M asked if K knew CPR. K said no, but Q did. M told K to phone Q. K pressed 4 on speed dial. Q was in a meeting but took the call anyway. K explained I had collapsed. Stay calm, Q said, remove any dangerous objects from the area, and call emergency. K said the phone was tied up and that M would have to use the land-line downstairs. M went to call 911. In the meantime, Q instructed K to check for breathing by turning the head face up, with the forehead tilted back and the chin lifted. K put down the phone and performed the procedure. K told Q I wasn't breathing. M returned and said an ambulance was coming. Q told K to tell M to begin mouth-to-mouth immediately. M grimaced and looked at K. K and I had dated once, so M thought K should do it. K said that was a long time ago, but OK. M took the phone. Q told M to tell K to pinch the nostrils while holding the chin in the other hand, place against the mouth, making a tight seal, then to gently exhale for about one to one and a half seconds. K complied. I still wasn't breathing. Try again, M said. Q said if that doesn't work, check for a pulse on the carotid artery in the neck. M told K. K didn't detect a heartbeat. M told Q there was no pulse and looked at K. K took the phone from M and asked Q what to do. If there is no pulse, begin chest compressions by placing the heel of one hand in the spot on the lower chest where the two halves of the rib cage come together, then put one hand on top of the other, interlocking the fingers, Q said. K explained the procedure to M. Q told K to tell M to make sure the breastbone only sinks about 1.5 to 2 inches, then to relieve the pressure. M asked K how many times. K asked Q. Q said to repeat the compressions about 16 times with 12- to 16-second intervals. M was in the middle of the procedure when the ambulance arrived. K hung up on Q and watched as the paramedics took over. M told K not to worry, that I was a survivor. K nodded. Then I was hoisted on to a stretcher and rushed to the hospital, where at 10:15AM, I was declared dead on arrival.

The Epiphany

K was certain the train-weight chain was obstructed and told M to check the adjacent frames and furniture. There are no interfering objects, M said. Perhaps the exterior surface is warped and is causing the chain to catch on the hole. Examine the case and repair any obvious defects, K said. Q nodded and examined the case. The surface around the hole was warped. Q drilled a larger hole for the train-weight chain. Now check to see if the chain is placed on the sprocket correctly, K said. M tugged the chain. If it moves and there is a clicking sound, then the chain is working, K said. M tugged the chain again. There is neither sound nor movement, M said. K said Ah ha, put the chain back on the sprocket. Q removed the back panel of the case. M looped the chain around the correct sprocket. Q replaced the panel. Now set the dials for 10:14, K said. M set the dials. Q looked at K. K raised an index finger. Cuckoo, I said.

Guggenheim

	I	K	M	Q
Metal bands	Iskra	Kataklysm	Morgoth	Quo Vadis
Kyoto signatories	Iraq	Kyrgysztan	Myanmar	Quatar
Quakers	Inaz	Kingsley	Mullins	Quare
Insults	Imperialist	Kunstler	Moron	Quanker

The Rules

Q turned off the device and rose to address the Chair. There are several upcoming scenarios that may be of interest to this committee, Q said. Please explain, I said. In "Felicity Conditions," four characters must negotiate a complex social situation in which there is a violation of a mutually agreed upon code. K rose. Is this the one where Mr. Roper overhears Jack and Chrissy in the kitchen and thinks they're doing it, when in fact they're only trying to stuff the Christmas turkey, K asked. I looked at Q. No, said Q, that is *Three's Company*. Because the only reason Jack is allowed to live with Chrissy and Janet is because Mr. Roper believes he's gay, K said. That is true, I said, but that does not concern this committee. M disagreed. Any performance which brings into full view the contours of a language game is of interest to this committee, M said. K nodded. I made a note about language games in the minutes. Q continued. In "Impossible Heap," a scene from Beckett's *Endgame* is appropriated and recast. K rose again. Is it that awful story about the Tailor? Yes, said Q. What does that mean, K asked. That means nothing, Q said. K looked at M. Shall I tell the story, M said. Please don't, I said.

Our *Words Are* Not Our *Words*

I received a letter from K two days after K received a package. In the letter K explained what Q had heard from M, that I had sent K the package. It was two days after I received the letter from K that K took the package to M to open. Q heard from M what K had told M two days before, that I had received a letter from K. K said I sent the package because of the return address M used on the box. I learned later that K received a package containing a device. K thought I was the sender because K saw the address M used on the package. K showed M what I had not sent two days before. M claimed to not recognize the address. But I knew that Q also had a letter from M using the return address I used. Q has admitted that the device had been sent in a package by M to K. M put the return address I used on the box for K to see, and then told K to take the package to Q. Two days after the package was received by K was the day I received the letter. So the fact that K received a package with same address I used does not prove that I was the sender.

Felicity Conditions

K placed a bowl of humous on the table, removed the plastic wrap, and cut the pita bread. Have some humous, K said. M picked up a piece of bread and dipped it in the bowl. This is good humous, said M. I nodded. Good, said K. Next, M brought out a bowl of salad. Have some salad, M said. I took a large serving. M served Q and K. The salad is very good, Q said. Good, said M. Lettuce is the key. Q looked at K. When the salad bowl was empty, Q went to the kitchen, removed a clay pot from the oven, and brought it to the table. Pork, said Q. I looked at M. M looked at K. That humous sure was filling, K said. M nodded. For a vegetarian dish, humous is surprisingly rich, M said. All that oil and tahini, I said. Not to mention the delicious and substantial bread, M added. A meal in itself, I said. Perhaps the pork should cool for a little while, K said. Great idea, take it outside, M said. Q looked at the table. I looked at K. This is a great party, K said. Sure is, said M. How about a round of Guggenheim, I said.

Impossible Heap

M told Q the story of K and the Tailor. K needed a pair of trousers in a hurry and went to a tailor. The tailor takes the measurements, and says come back in four days, the pants will be ready. Four days later K returns. So sorry, says the tailor, come back in a week, there's a problem with the seat. K says fine, an irregular seat would be very uncomfortable. Q nodded. M continued. A week later K returns to pick up the pants. Frightfully sorry, come back in ten days, the crotch is too small, the tailor says. Fine, a snug crotch is never pleasing, K replies. Ten days pass. Dreadfully sorry, come back in a fortnight, the fly is broken. K nodded, an open fly is truly an embarrassment. At the next visit, the tailor has ruined the buttonholes. Now K is angry. In six days, says K, God made the world — the WORLD. And yet it takes one tailor three months to make a simple pair of trousers. But K, says the Tailor, look at the world — then look at these trousers. M stopped and stared at Q. Q was impassive, eyes unseeing. M broke into a high forced laugh, cut it short, turned towards Q, and launched into laughter again. Silence, I yelled. Will this never finish?

The Party

Q wanted to communicate a message. M told Q that before a message could be communicated, the sender had to consider the purpose of the message. What is the purpose of this message, M asked. What are the choices, Q replied. To persuade, to entertain, to inform, or to express emotions, M said. Or to deceive, I added. M looked at K. K looked at Q. The purpose of this message is to inform, Q said. Good, said M. Now describe the values and interests of the audience that will receive the message, K said. Q asked why. K explained that a message has to be sent in a form that the audience will find appealing. I grimaced. What if the audience doesn't exist yet, I asked. Q looked at M. The sender must imagine that the audience exists, M said. I looked at K. K looked at the clock. Q was imagining the values and interests of the pretend audience. The clock struck 10:15. Is it time to communicate now, Q asked. K and M nodded. But before Q could begin, I had to ask why the question of audience had once again subsumed the problem of form.

How To

I watched as K closed the distance between M and Q. First, K rotated around the knob, tightening after each revolution. M flanked while Q reamed the burr. Q took care not to damage K. Then K covered M with tape. Q worked at the low end as I continued to watch. M drained Q completely. Once the fluid had drained out, K stuffed something white in. K told M to polish the last inch down to the shoulder. Q applied some flux around the pip. I felt the heat from the bottom as M passed back and forth, distributing everything evenly. I was told to take care not to get too hot, and not to stick. I wanted to touch the joint occasionally, to avoid overheating. But M thought I wasn't ready. M moved to the edge and pulled Q in with capillary action. K told M to be certain there were no gaps. It was some time later that I wiped off the excess flux with a damp rag, leaving small traces in each of the crevices.

Title

K owned property. I wanted to purchase property. Q and M were agents. K told Q property was for sale. Q went to meet K to assess the value of the property. Q told K the asking price should be $248,000. K had paid $160,000 five years earlier and told Q that was great. Q took photographs of the property. I saw the photographs and phoned M. M confirmed that the property was available and that I could view it. M contacted Q to arrange a showing. Q did not respond. M called Q thee times and thought that Q was trying to create a buzz. I told M that was a problem. So M phoned K directly. Then K phoned Q. Q was not happy about M and K being in direct contact. M received a call from Q immediately. Q said that M had broken protocol by contacting K. M and I didn't care so long as I was the first to view the property. So M, Q and I met at the property without K. The property was just like the photographs. I told M that I would pay $240,000. M wrote an offer and gave it to Q. Q gave the offer to K and K accepted. But that was not the end. There were subjects that both K and I had to have removed. K wanted a deposit of $40,000 but I didn't have the money. I had to get financing. I also had to arrange to have the property inspected. In the meantime, I wanted K to pump out the septic, but K needed to sell the property first. Q was keyed up, M was cautiously optimistic, K was distrustful, and I was tense. Then the subjects were removed. In the end, K took the money, Q and M took a commission, and I took possession of the title.

The One That Got Away

M, Q, K, and I were out early last Monday morning, using green spackleback hoochies and a few tiny strips. The wind was blowing northwest 24 knots. Tucked in by the green can off Thrasher to get a bit of shade, Q ran the boat up into the wind and had just turned around when a fish tripped off the downrigger. I pulled the slack and handed the rod to K. M and Q started clearing the gear on the other side of the boat. Halfway up and a bigger Chinook hit. The fish ran about 224 yards of line. K figured there may have been 24 yards left on the reel when Q turned the fish. I got the first fish up to the boat after 12 minutes, put the rod in the holder, and helped M to net another fish off the port. It was a nice fish, but M clubbed it fast and got it out of the way so the big one could be landed. Twenty-four minutes later it was still 16 yards from the boat. K was tiring rapidly, and pointed the rod at the fish. The big one split the hook and was up in the air before heading down under the boat. Now the fish M landed weighed in at 48 pounds, so I reckon the big one that got away weighed at least 64.

Clock

Q tied a 4-foot length of string into a loop and attached it to K. K curled around the front and wrapped it tight. Q repeated the motion, picking up the string lying across. Cat's cradle, K said. I nodded. Next M pulled the crossed strings out, above the parallel ones, pushing them up through the centre. Q stretched and pulled taut against K. Soldier's bed, I said. Q pulled the crossed strings out, above the parallel ones, and pushed them up through the centre a second time. K and Q stretched apart. Candles, I said. M pulled the inner strands to opposite sides of the figure. Q scooped under the double strings and K held taut. Manger, I said. M pulled the crossed strings out under parallel ones, then over and down the centre. Q stretched apart and pulled the string taut. Cat's eye, Q said. No, Diamonds, I said. Q nodded. M pinched interwoven strings from the top, then pivoted. Q and K pulled apart. Fish in a dish, I said. Q pinched crossed strings and pivoted upward. K and Q stretched the strings taut. K looked at Q. Q looked at the string. What is this, M asked. Clock, I said, though I knew it had another name.

I Had a Dream

I was in a small room overlooking the principal square of a foreign town when the clock in the room next door struck the quarter hour. In the centre of the square, a threatening statue of Wittgenstein stood upon a plinth. The light was fading as I watched K contemplate the statue from a table in the eastern quarter of the square. I was vaguely aware of strange sounds rising from the gloomy streets. M entered the square, followed by Q. M crossed the square and took a seat at the table. Q followed. Now Q was turned away from M and K but was observing the scene through a reflection in an adjacent window. A faint smell of the docks hung in the air, giving the scene an atmosphere of tedium, melancholy and anguish. At this exact moment, I recalled a certain dream in which K, M, and Q were breaking light bulbs on a wall. When I looked closer, K had the eyes of a fish, M the head of a pig, and Q was posing as the Queen of Diamonds. Lost in this vision, I failed to notice that K, M, and Q had left the scene, and that the square was once again empty.

Sous les Pavés

K hurled a garbage can through the doors of the Bay. M dragged a newspaper box into the street, doused it in nail polish remover, and lit it on fire. Q kicked in the windshield on a Honda Element and removed a device. Cops, pigs, murderers, I said. K masked up and entered the store. M knocked a CTV camera to the ground. Journalists are cops, M said. Break the police occupation, Q said. I removed a can of spray paint from a backpack and wrote CIVIL WAR in front of the TD Bank. K emerged from the Bay with boxes of perfume and tossed them into the crowd. M kicked in the door of Le Chateau and ran inside. Q followed M. I merged with the crowd. K was singing. M came out of Le Chateau with a cash register. Q was wearing four leather jackets. I joined a group trying to overturn a CBC van. K was there too. M threw the cash register into Blenz. Suddenly the police charged on horses. Q shed three jackets and ran towards the subway. I grabbed a jacket and started walking east. K took another jacket, changed into a new pair of shoes, and headed to the library. M picked up the last jacket and went for frozen yogurt in the mall. Later that night, I updated Facebook: "wonderful day on the beach."

Nothing to Lose

M fingered the chips and sighed, hoping to feign weakness, then pushed the pile into the middle of the table. K called the raise and bumped it $6,400. I lit a cigarette, counted the stack, and speculated on how Q would play it. K didn't bother because of a nice pair of aces, but if Q called, the flop would change everything. And Q had the advantage: K was all-in so there was no more betting. Q decided five-four was worth the small dent it would make in the forty-some-thousand on the table, and played the ace and queen of diamonds. When K replied with the two black aces, there was a buzz around the table. I gave M a look. Slow-playing aces was either the height of cheek, or of idiocy. At any rate, K was out. The flop brought a black queen, giving Q a useless pair, and the last thing M wanted to see: two small diamonds, making four to a flush. There was an irrelevant seven of spades, then I played the fifth and final card, which would determine the future: the ten of diamonds. That made the flush. M went pale. Once again I had defied the odds, and once again I held the title.

In Our Beginning Is Our End

Q placed the corner poles at right angles to the established survey lines. K and I marked the corners of line *A*. The length of side C was specified in the plans and could not be changed. M calculated the length of side Z by adding together the square of side *A* and the square of side B. Z was equal to the square root of that sum ($Z = \sqrt{A^2 + B^2}$). Once M had deduced that number, I attached a piece of tape equal in length to Z to Q, and another piece equal to *A* to K. The point where both tapes were stretched tight indicated the location for X. Q then used the same method M had used to locate the spot for Y. When Y was placed, Q announced that the design was complete and that it was finally time to build the foundation. But as I tried to square the base by stretching another piece of tape between two diagonally opposite poles, it became clear that this project could proceed no further.

Index of First Lines

Acknowledgements

Selections from IKMQ have appeared in *The Capilano Review*, *Matrix*, PRECIPICE, and *West Coast Line*. Thanks to Jenny Penberthy, Anne Stone, Adam Dickinson, Gregory Betts, Michael Barnholden, and Glen Lowry.

Thanks also to Dianna Bonder, for giving me a space to work; to Neil Kelly, for lending me his two-volume edition of *How Things Work: The Universal Encylopedia of Machines* (Palladin, 1974) at exactly the right moment; and to Zoë Lamb, whose eye for surface and line helps me to write better.

I would also like to acknowledge the support of the Canada Council for the Arts, which provided a grant that assisted in the composition and revision of this book.

FSC
www.fsc.org
RECYCLED
Paper made from recycled material
FSC® C100212